Pathos   Love   Comedy

II

PATHOS * LOVE * COMEDY

A Book of Verse

by

Sheila Miller

Published in 1995 by REAL LIFE PUBLISHING
P.O. Box 74,
Grimsby,
Lincolnshire
DN35 0XA

All Rights Reserved

ISBN No....0 9526422 0 4

Copytype and Artwork by David Miller Services

Photo Printed and Bound in Great Britain by

ALBERT GAIT LTD

Castle Press

Grimsby,

Lincolnshire

The right of Sheila Miller to be identified as the sole author of this work has been asserted in accordance with the Copyright, Designs and Patents Act 1988.

No verse, paragraph or lyric of this publication to be copied or transmitted save with written permission or in accordance with the provisions of the Copyright Act of 1956 as amended.

British Library Cataloguing in Publication Data.

A catalogue record for this book is available from the British Library

Sheila Miller is from a Grimsby family with a fishing tradition. She is a lyricist and composer and has co-written with and been recorded by the Internationally famous singer, writer and film star Charles Aznavour. She has been writing in some form or another since the seventies and has been published in several anthologies This is her first collection of verse and lyrics on life and relationships. Sheila enjoys singing, and is a former member of the Ladies Barbershop Harmony Chorus The Humber Belles. She is a member of PRS and BASCA and an Undergraduate Student with the Open University.

This Book Is Dedicated To
My Son Guy And His Wife Jayne

And In Memory Of Champion

*I try to walk in others shoes
Understand the way they feel
And then I put my simple views
Of how it seems to me
I cannot touch another's heart
Or get inside their head
Neither can I catch the joy
Or weep the tears they shed
But if I seem to comprehend
In this book for you
The memories, dreams, the sense of fun
Of even just a few
Then I am glad for I'll have done
What I set out to do.*

Sheila Miller

Special thanks to Peter Diamond
For his kindness, help and enthusiasm

CONTENTS

Page

1	She's Gone
2	A Mother
3	This Afternoon
4	Letters
5	Without You
6	Love The Innocent Years
7	Dark Side Of The Street
8	The Letter
9	Lonely Hearts
10	Has Your Town
11	Intercity
12	The Prolapse
13	The Doctor
14	Compassion
15	Claude
16	When I Was A Kid
17	Break The Silence
18	Love
19	Heaven Only Knows
20	Love Story
21	Life
22	Socks
23	Second Best
24	Dreams
25	Treasures
26	Funny Guy
27	That Was Happiness-That Was
28	Song For Ken
29	Summertime
30	Love Thoughts
31	What About The Children
32	Fags
34	All Kinds Of Love

CONTENTS

Page

36	*Highrise*
37	*Love And War*
38	*My Life*
39	*Hangups*
40	*You Could Be The One*
41	*Trust Me*
42	*The Clown*
43	*The Flower*
44	*Chains*
45	*Waiting*
46	*Nobody's Fault*
47	*Northern Lass*
48	*After A Lifetime*
49	*I Heard A Voice*
50	*When You're Out Of My Sight*
51	*Bridge Of Time*
52	*Skeletons*
53	*Your Mind*
54	*The Writer*
55	*Time For Me Time For You*
56	*Home And Free*
57	*All On An April Evening*
58	*Plastic Friends*
59	*The Pools Winner*
60	*Yesterday*
61	*The Bridge*
62	*Who Was The Child?*
63	*A Thought*
64	*Land Of Strangers*
65	*He*
66	*The Attic*

CONTENTS

Page

67	*The Lost*
68	*Maggie*
69	*Lily*
70	*Tears*
71	*The Beach*
72	*Son*
73	*The Photograph*
74	*Children*
75	*Letter From A Soldier*
76	*I Wish I'd Known Then*
77	*Shag Connors*
78	*Brother Wonderful*
79	*Heart*
80	*Boxes*
82	*Walls*
83	*All That Christmas Means*
84	*The Visitor*
86	*Quiet Man*
87	*Everyone's A Poet*
88	*Every Now And Then*
89	*The Performer*
90	*Just A Phase*
91	*Was It Love*
92	*The Search*
94	*They Shall Have Loving*
95	*Mirrors*
96	*Him and Me*
98	*Be Yourself*

SHE'S GONE.

When you wake she will be gone
The bed her side not laid upon
She's going out to find the sun
She's been the stranger for so long

You'll read her letter stained with tears
Then know her smile's the mask she wears
To hide her lonliness, her fears
Did you not know in all these years?

Did you not see the warning signs?
The silent breakfast, morning times
Two souls apart, in heart and minds
Could you not read between the lines?

I heard you say, she wasn't tied,
She always seemed so satisfied
She loved her home, it was her pride
She loved you too, until it died

You'll read with unsuspecting eyes
Her touching words and realise
We should hear the caged bird's cries
Long before she soars and flies.

A MOTHER.

Through the pains of birth
'Til they see the light of day
Through their morning years
And when they've flown away
And you're worrying inside
And sometimes cannot hide the tears
Then the night becomes your friend
'Til another day begins
And you smile and play pretend

You want it all for them
But you cannot give it
You cannot teach them life
They must learn it as they live it

Living up to a mother's role
Can wear you down
'Til you feel old
So.....when you put on your face today
And smile,
And when you say "I'm fine"
Don't worry
We will read between the lines.

THIS AFTERNOON

This afternoon,
I am remembering
Repeating to myself, well spoken vows
This afternoon
Imagining
Repeating promises forgotten now

She's beautiful,
I am so proud
And I know deep inside you are proud too
And it's so right
That I should be here
To give our girl away
This afternoon

You're close to me,
And as I gaze at you
My eyes are misty with the mingled tears
How could our love
Just fade away
After all those tender years

You're smiling now,
But I can see,
Completely out of reach you are to me
I kiss the bride
And feel inside
A father's pride touch jealousy

I catch your eye,
Our daughter throws her rose bouquet
High into the sky,
As our eyes meet
In memories
Bitter sweet
This afternoon

LETTERS

We were young
And in love
When he left
Saying
"I'll write you soon with my address"
Forty years on
Of wondering and whying
She handed to me
My mother now dying
Love letters that told
Of the life I'd have lived
Held my hands worn and ringless
And said
"Daughter .....forgive"

WITHOUT YOU

Without you, what am I
I'm the sky without the sun
To bring the morning on
I'm the rainbow without the rain
That no one ever sees
I'm the melody
Sleeping on the breeze

Without you what am I
I'm the night without the day
With no light to take the dark away
I'm a name without a face
I'm a ghost without a resting place
I'm the tide that never turns
I'm the lesson no one ever learns

And without you
I could never reach that brightest star
You are my reason to go on
Without you
I'm a picture - sad
With no one to paint a smile upon.

LOVE THE INNOCENT YEARS

A child sees a colour
It's so much brighter
A child sees a snowflake
It's so much whiter
A little child's heart
Is so much lighter
Love the innocent years

A child makes a friend
When he may have none
On his friend he'll depend
Be glad he's sent one
But if his friend goes
Then he'll invent one
Love the innocent years.

A child may be lonely
And never show it
A child may be lonely
You may not know it
Take care with your love
And where you throw it
Love the innocent years

DARK SIDE OF THE STREET

Life comes cheap on City Streets
On the tinsel mile that never sleeps
Teenage dreamers, on the hook
Walk the wires
Eyes like fires
And lust for Angel Dust

A kid alone gets stoned and finds
The kialeidascope that blows his mind
He walks the Maze
Easy meat
On the dark side of the Street

The shadows hide a young girl's shame
Sells body and soul to feed the vein
Buy one more day's
Sweet deceit
On the dark side of the street

To curious eyes, the City shines
But the neon lights can strike you blind
To misery
Beyond belief
On the dark side of the street.

THE LETTER.

*She wrote a letter to herself
It wasn't disapproving
It wasn't cold, it didn't scold
No, it was very moving
It said :-*

*I've known you all my life
Once I looked on you in shame
I didn't like the secret you
I didn't like your name
And all the mirrors in the world
Assuming they were true
Told me things about you
Things that others never knew
Years and years of crouching down
Spine and shoulders bent
Face all furrowed in a frown
Of obvious discontent
Silent tears just crying out
When no one listened to
The simple signs of your self doubt
And so it grew and grew
Then looking through a glass one day
You thought was telling lies
You saw the image of yourself
Through optimistic eyes
You stood confident and tall
Beside an opened door
You came on through
And left behind
The mask that once you wore
Now all the mirrors in this world
Whatever they may say
They cannot change the you
You've grown into today
And as I close this letter
With all my love I send
It's good to know you now, at last*

*Sincerely,
        Your Best Friend.*

LONELY HEARTS.

When those sugar words
Have turned to salty tears
And you feel it's time
For you to shine
Bury the past
But not too fast
Be sure it's dead
Before you look ahead
Then.... Dress your days in dreams
And think of me when the music starts
In memory of the lonely hearts.

HAS YOUR TOWN

Has your town got a Precinct
Where everybody shops?
And has it got a car park
That goes up and up and up?
And has it got a Woolies
And a Marks and C & A?
And has it got a fountain
And a place here kiddies play?
And has it a Mc Donalds
Or a good old Wimpy Bar?
And has it got a Card Shop
Sells trinkies for your car?
And has it got a Mr Minit
And a Boots and M.F.I.?
And has it got just everything
You're itching for to buy?
And has it got some litter bins
Sometimes get unused?
And has it got some coppers
That sometimes get abused?
And those with walkie talkies
Always making calls?
And has it some toilets
With no graffiti on the walls?.
Well I'd love to come and see it
To get a change of scene
But what's the use of turning up
In the place that I've just been.

INTERCITY

The weather's nice
For early May
I travelled down just for the day
There amongst the crowd I stop and pause
For a magic moment near the City stores
The windows full of models going round and round
I hear the buskers playing near the Underground
I ride the escalators up and down
To all the floors
And think of all I'm going to spend
On my favourite worthy cause
I make believe a limousine
With chauffeur handsome tall and lean
Waits for me to open up the doors
I cannot take in everything because
I'm enchanted by the busy City stores

THE PROLAPSE

My mother's got a prolapse
Or so the Doctor. said
She's got to go in hospital
When they can find a bed
I gather something's outside
That really should be in
So either they'll remove it
Or push it back again
I know sometimes it pains her
And I know sometimes it smarts
I think she should go private
As it's in her private parts
But she is not in BUPA
And she won't have the knife
Tho' if she had the lucre
I'm sure she'd have it twice
So as she don't have the money
And they don't have the time
For now she's walking funny
And drinking too much wine
I've seen her doing hand stands
For gravity to win
And cursing when she stands up
And loses it again
I've even seen her turn round
When walking down the street
To see if she has dropped it
Somewhere around her feet
My mother's got a prolapse
I said "I tell you what
Forget about the hospital
Go to the body shop".

THE DOCTOR

I am here to treat the sporty
The under and the over forty
The naughty and the not so naughty
And all those in between
I treat the mums who've just conceived
I treat the lonely and bereaved
Treat the worried and the peeved
The streetwise and the green
Visit them inside their home
Pacify them on the phone
When they want to pick a bone
I see them as and when
Examine them when they are fit
To get a job or take a trip
Soothe them when they hurt a bit
With my magic pen
I don't pretend I'm what I 'aint
I'm a Doctor, not a Saint
I listen well to each complaint
The big ones and the smalls
When on me they do descend
Be it backs that will not bend
Or fronts and sides that will not mend
Or even be it balls.

COMPASSION.

There's no pretence
He lives his life to share
A heart as sensative as this is rare
But the world's too big, too wide
It's sad he cannot hide
His pain for others needing sympathy
He cares for children even as his own
Carries others burdens on his back alone
But soon he will break
He is no superman
He can take no more than any other can
He loves the world so tenderly
The animals, people, birds
But to suffer for all is impossible
And if he reads these words
I just want to say ,
If he should go away
We would miss him
We would miss him.

CLAUD

He went to Church to pray
One December Sunday day
Only he and God knows now
The words he had to say
Alone he climbed the high belltower
He chose to spend his final hour
With those understanding Hosts
The Father, Son, and Holy Ghost
He wasn't Tennyson or Keats
This gentle soul, but thoughts I'll keep
Of a poet just like me
Of sharing once our poetry
And everytime the Church bells ring
Me, I shall remember him.

WHEN I WAS A KID.

*I saw too much I did, when I was a kid
I saw too much, but couldn't tell a soul
But then who would believe me if I told
You know, I'd like to say I ran away
But no, I had to stay there in that Hell
With all those secrets that I couldn't tell*

*I heard too much I did, when I was a kid
I heard too much, too much for little ears
I learned to play my part and hide my tears
Well, I can still recall the little me
Inside my fantasies where I would hide
And in that mean world, I learned to survive*

*I gave too much I did, when I was a kid
I gave my word, be seen and not be heard
And still would you believe nobody cared
You know I'd like to say that's far away
But I'm still stuck today, Oh God forbid
With all those secrets, when I was a kid.*

BREAK THE SILENCE

Dig deep
Unearth the memories that sleep
Face the monsters, long delayed
So to rest they may be laid.....for
Crammed inside the mind so long
Just think, they cannot be that strong
They've not been aired, they cannot breathe
Who does not know them they deceive
Let them out, they that lie
Do not fear the tears you cry
Break the silence, free the soul
See the monsters lose control
They once seething in your head
Will drown in all the tears you shed.

LOVE

Love is beauty, love is blind
Love is joyful, love is kind
Love is sorrow borne with grace
Love is helping every race
Love is hurting really deep
Love is soothing whilst two sleep
Love is helping all to learn
Love seeks nothing in return
Love is tearful for the young
Love's a song with meaning sung
Love is humble, love is sure
Love is easier when mature
Love is not a sacrifice
Love is everything that's nice
Love is colour all around
Love is every single sound
Love is home where comfort reigns
Love isn't just a passion flame
Love is all the air we breathe
Love remains when we all leave.

HEAVEN ONLY KNOWS

Why are Heavens Gates called Pearly?
Why are some folks taken early?
Why do some not go, just nearly?
Heaven only knows

Why is life sometimes a feast
To the folks who have the least?
Why does man become a priest?
Heaven only knows

Why do those with true belief
Ride the storms and hide the grief?
Smiles outside and tears beneath
Heaven only knows

Time divides regrets - content
Wisdom comes as life is spent
What will be the main event?
Heaven only knows.

LOVE STORY.

I was eighteen I remember,
When she brought him home that time
He was standing by the window
I was wishing he was mine
As the three of us ate supper
His eyes never left my eyes
For to him I was a woman
But to her I was a child

And he knew what I was feeling
And I knew he felt the same
Oh I knew how much she loved him
And she'd lost one loving game
But there's no one on this earth
Could have kept us far apart
We had to have each other
Break another woman's heart

I love my mother's lover
I'm taking him away
For I cannot go without him
And I cannot bear to stay
We're leaving in the morning
For a far and distant shore
I'll write her that I love her
But I love her lover more

She is young enough to make out
And I'm old enough to leave
And you know, she always told me
If you find someone you need
Show him how he's loved and wanted
And that is what I've done
But I wish my mother's lover
Hadn't been the one.

LIFE.

*They gave you the world on a silver platter
But that kind of love is a crime
When they took it away,
Like a child with a toy
I watched you cry,
Like a lost little boy
And I wanted to hold you
For I could have told you
This was the way it would be
Well, I had the dreams
And you had the power
Each one I lost
All it cost me was time
'Though you'd never known
What it's like to go hungry
I wouldn't have traded your life for mine
Now what you do best
You're no longer sure of
Your dream world is empty
The phone rings no more
Oh you've so much to learn
But no one can teach you
'Cause life is a lesson
There're no teachers for
Now the path that you follow
To that unknown tomorrow
Is the one I have followed
With no one to lead
That road I would wander
But returned even stronger
Never losing my hunger
To try and succeed
So go seek and find you
And don't look behind you
Just follow the night
And when you reach the end
Then look for the marker
At the place where it's darker
And know that I've been there
And come back again
Then know me much better
And know I'm you're friend.*

SOCKS.

My God, every single one is odd
I buy a pair, both matching shades
One disappears, or one just fades
I buy some more, start fresh and clean
Scrutinise my washing machine
Put them in two by two
Guard them with my life for you
Dry them, air them, but come to pair them
I wish that I could promise you
There won't be one instead of two.

SECOND BEST

*Why am I the one
Always in hot water?
Why aren't I your son
Instead of just your daughter?
I didn't ask to be
I know it is a shame
A boy you wanted first
But I am not to blame
So you got second best
You didn't get the prize
Want to know the truth?
With me the same applies
But as you're stuck with me
And I am stuck with you
We'll have to do the best
That all of us can do
And if you love me more
Than you ever thought you could
Next time God may grant your wish
For being extra good.*

DREAMS

My dreams were big when I was small
To some they were not dreams at all
A bedtime story, a goodnight kiss
An unbroken promise, a granted wish
Afterschool playfriends, no more alone
A holiday to a happy home
I'm not small now
Still, my dreams are big
I wish all of this
For every kid.

TREASURES.

I was invited to her coffee morning
Her garden a picture around the bright awning
What a wonderful way she did entertain
We moved to the house when it started to rain

Her guests were so varied as I can recall
There hung a Van Gogh on the drawing room wall
I loved her Victorian dolls and porcelain
I mingled awhile and she said "glad you came"

As I took my leave and I drove down the road
I thought I'd invite her to my humble abode
I'd seen her fine treasures and it made me sigh
For she had so much, but then so did I.

I rang her next day, at once she accepted
Not knowing exactly what she expected
I invited my friends, close since I was a child
Through marriage and children, and divorce long since filed

And then as we waited, I looked round the room
My wall plaque, a sunset to brighten the gloom
The doll from my childhood, and most precious of all
My son's crayon picture pinned up on the wall

When my new guest arrived my nervousness gone
I lined up more treasures, I'd had for so long
She smiled, understood, and shook hands with each one.

FUNNY GUY

*You never learned to wrap up
From the bitter winds
Well everybody knows
It takes all kinds
To make up this world
Of might have beens
You're a funny guy*

*You never learned to turn off
When the trouble comes
Never learned to separate your mind
Never walk away
'til the troubles done
You're a funny guy*

*Still we stick together
You and I
Carry one another when things get rough
Seems to me though sometimes
You can't get enough
Of drifting
You keep changing with the wind
And biting at the hand of fate
You never seem to get it straight*

*You don't see tomorrow
Take sorrow in your stride
Every nights a Beano
Life's a bumpy ride
Don't get me wrong now
You have pride
Back of this is where you hide*

*You wake up in the mornings
Out on the streets
Can't remember where
You spent the night
Hands in your pockets
A gleam in your eye
You're a funny guy*

THAT WAS HAPPINESS - THAT WAS.

What is happiness?
I've become aware
We don't always know
Exactly what it is
Until it isn't there

Noisy home with cluttered toys
Friday nights out with the boys
Home to face the angry wife
That was happiness that was

Kids around me everywhere
Dog forever in my chair
Nothing could I call my own
That was happiness that was

Saturdays reserved for me
Sundays for the family
Shame you know I couldn't see
That that was happiness that was

Close we were the kids and me
Oh my friends what fools are we
To think our needs are to be free
Well, that was happiness that was.

No one now for company
Just memories of a girl and me
The girl I loved became my wife
And now, she is out of my life

She, my kids, my family
Now they are even more to me
And what I thought was compromise
Well, that was happiness that was.

SONG FOR KEN.

One sweet summer long
You and he were one
He came to decorate your life
It should have been forever
And if he were here
He would kiss you better
And wipe away your tears
But he won't let you be
In shadows of the night
I look at you and see
He still shines so bright
And even though he's gone
And Winters seem so long
So you could make it through
He left his light with you

And even though someday
There'll be another song
When your journey's done
This will be the one.

For Gill

SUMMERTIME

Autumn leaves, falling from the trees
Cover misty summer memories
When we touched the stars
Before you left
December in my heart

And today, like a summer breeze
As I read simple words you write to me
Soft your voice, inside my mind
Whisper words of love between the lines

I can't forget how you changed my life
All it took was one Summer night
I can't forget all your dreams were mine
When all our days were Summertime

I recall as the Seasons change
Standing here in the sad remains
Those nights you made me shine
And misty mornings
When the world was yours and mine
And wish us both an Indian Summertime

LOVE THOUGHTS

Some people go looking for love
But is love something
You can seek and find?
And then won't it depend
On your frame of mind?
Is love attraction,
Or the re-action to attraction?
Is love physical or is it mental?
Is it powerful or is it gentle?
And how do you know
If it's love when you find it?
A passionate night
Can have so much behind it?
Some people love
And they never know it
Some people love
And can never show it
Some people show it
But then they blow it
Some think they cannot
Live without it
Some have so much love,
Yet they doubt it
But love
Is each one's own perception
Whatever their faith,
Their thoughts, their direction
And brave are the steps
Into the unknown
But happy the heart
That finds it's home

WHAT ABOUT THE CHILDREN?

Most of us good people
Are pretty much the same
We do our very best
And we hope for some acclaim
We all have our ways
Of playing life's game
But what about our children?

Almost all life stories
Are tinged with some regret
Some bordering the perfect
Most trying hard to get
The love and harmony
We all come to respect
But what about our children?

Some of us good people
We colour all our past
We make it what it isn't
For we have to make it last
We make the colours bright
When life is overcast
But what about our children?

Most of us good people
We evaluate our lives
We tie things up real neat
And whoever may survive
Perpetuates the myth
So generations sigh
What about the children?

FAGS.

He used to smoke plenty
He used to smoke twenty
Then thirty, then forty a day
His missus was houseproud
And boy she would nag
He'd scowl and he'd whisper`
"You silly old hag"
And when she said "Pardon!"
He'd lie, "got a fag"
As he slipped his packet away
She tried hard to stop him
From fouling the house
She used disinfectant
He'd grunt and he'd grouse
But he still spent his day
With a fag in his mouth
She'd rant and she'd rave
And she begged him to save
His money, his life
Her love as his wife
But he was addicted
And that made him mean
The more he would puff
The more she would scream
He dotted his ashes
All over the floor
She'd hoover and hoover
Then open the door
To let out his smoke
And let off her steam
As the smoke rings had faded
Well so had her dream
He said he'd give up
When she threatened to leave him
She didn't, he did,
Next day, he stopped breathing

*And when his cremation
Was over at last
The guy who was known,
For dropping his ash
Would rest in his urn
On the desk by the door
'Til one day it fell
And slipped on the floor
His widow in mourning
Houseproud to the last
Switched on the hoover
And cleaned him up fast.*

ALL KINDS OF LOVE.

We are men of the world, you and I understand
But I am what I am
We are father and son, we are closer than some
So I speak man to man
And your mother and me, deeper love there can't be
Yet between you and me
Once before you were born, feeling bad I left home
When she walked over me

There're all kinds of love
And there're all kinds of fools
She would not give in, I could not be used
Well I had to choose, and that's when I ran
For I had to prove, that I was a man.

It was Paris in France, I made love every chance
And I lived to the hilt
And I smothered my pain, in soft skin and perfume
And I lived with my guilt
I had friends, had a ball, I thought I was all
I wanted to be
'Til one day I woke up, and my friends had all gone
And I saw the real me

I was less than a man, less than when I began
And I felt so alone
I'd been living so well, on a bright carousel
That was all broken down
And the pride I would don, like a badge was now gone
Oh the nights were so cold
As I slept all alone, missed my family and home
And came back to the fold

There're all kinds of love
There're all kinds of fools
As blindly I drank the cup of my youth
My dominant one, I left for so long
Had mothered the you, that I never knew

And now you're in my shoes, one more faint hearted
 fool
You don't know how to choose
And it's not like they said, now you've found that
true love
Cannot not always run smooth
For your woman's headstrong, and she knows
What she wants
Well son all I can say
There're all kinds of fools, but the worst is the fool
Who keeps running away.

There're all kinds of love, we don't always see
 Woman and man
There's one love we're sure of, between you and me
Father and son

HIGH-RISE.

I hear my baby crying
I'm tired from not sleeping
Afraid if I stop trying
They'll not let me keep him
We live in Hightowers
Where you can't pick the flowers
And I'm looking down
Where the grass once green
Is trampled brown

Do they know we're here?
Do they know it's raining?
Baby, don't they know
You need a place to grow?

In our room with a view
A room for for just two
I cry my tears
These walls are thin
Yet no one hears

I'll get us out of here
I swear
As sure as the nightplane flies
And the midnight stars
Are lonely eyes
Look down, look down
To solid ground,
That's where you're bound
Now..... hold my hand.....
Say goodbye Highrise.

LOVE AND WAR

Give her a moment to ponder
Then wait for the light in her eyes
As back through the years she will wander
To the buttercup days of her life
Wait for the lilt of her laughter
As mem'ries sweet colour her cheeks
And watch for the sway
As she's humming away
The tunes of the days she now speaks
She'll tell you of joy in no measure
She'll tell of time, precious and brief
She'll keep some secrets safe,
Her own treasure
With the tears that she shed underneath

She'll talk of the day that she met him
Too young for a man's uniform
How she knew then she'd never forget him
How his son and heir was still born
She'll tell you her life
Since she lost him
No bitterness now in her tone
You can save all your pity, this lady
She knows she is never alone

She'll listen for bugles at morning
And retrace the steps that he trod
The farther the field,
And the years in between
Serve only to strengthen her love
He's clearer, and blonder, and closer
Than ever he was long before
They took those young lads
For the lambs then
And the fountain of youth won the war.

Give her a moment to ponder
Then wait for the light in her eyes
As back through the years she will wander
To the buttercup days of her life.

MY LIFE

I would like to make my life
Seem colourful and pretty
I would like my story
To be like a Walter Mitty
But I do hate to lie
And today is not right
For baring my soul
In just black and white
So if you don't mind
I guess I can wait
I'll compose myself
Then I'll compose my fate
And when I feel clever
Which I sometimes do
I'll garnish my story
For me, not for you
So that I can see it
Through a soft rosy hue.

HANGUPS.

*I watch 'em waiting for some lame dog
To come along
To need 'em and they feed 'em
And then they make 'em strong
Then they tag 'em
When they're done
"NOW YOU BELONG"
Some people need other peoples 'hangups*

*I've seen 'em searching for the sad ones
It's in their blood
They weed out all the bad ones
So they can make 'em good
Any old soul
And the young
Misunderstood
Some people need other peoples' hangups*

*I heard 'em praying for the lost ones
Getting high
Squeezing tears
From sad and lonely eyes*

*Now they are crying in the darkness,
'Oh Lord help me'
It's easy to work out - Hell!
How lonely they must be
I can't tell 'em
What I see
Oh No! not me
Some people need other peoples' hangups*

YOU COULD BE THE ONE

Speak your mind
You could find
Trouble
Lead the way
You could walk
Alone
Do not lie
Omit the truth
Don't be loud
Be aloof
Speak your mind
And you could be the one
The chopper falls upon.

TRUST ME

You've a story for to tell
So tell it all to me
I want to know it all friend
Way down your family tree
Tell me of your childhood
Of your mis-spent youth
I'll tell it so it sounds good
I'll only tell the truth
Tell me of your preference
Of your deep desires
I'll treat it with pure reverence
And as the law requires
You can't kiss and tell
To anyone but me
I'm true to the code
You know, of decency
What about some pictures
Climb upon the stool
We've got to make this good friend
Or I will look a fool
Tell me what's the name friend
Whom shall I accuse
Justify the noughts friend
For hyper front page news

THE CLOWN.

Behind the comic face is tragedy, nobody knows
Inside the heart so generous
Is emptiness and longing
Holding his tears at bay, keeping his cool
He's playing the fool, just long enough
To let the heartaches go away

The happiness he leaves behind him
Everywhere he goes
He leaves the stage and in his ears
The laughter is still ringing
Holding his fears at bay
Keeping his cool
He's playing the fool just long enough
To make the heartaches go away

The Prince of Clowns is what they call him
Artist of renown
To paint a face so joyful
 Nobody would guess
Behind the makeup
There's the emptiness and longing he works hard
In keeping up his facade of happiness

The Fool of fortune played his symphony
Long long ago
And in his head, the violins
Well, they're still playing
Casting his dreams away, keeping his cool
He's playing the fool just long enough
To make the heartaches go away

A little child presents a flower
To the Prince of Clowns
The flower says much more than any word could tell
Holding the child oh so tenderly
He takes another bow
Before he leaves again
To face his private Hell

THE FLOWER

I saw a path that I should walk
Was overgrown with weeds
I thought that I should clear them out
And plant some flower seeds
Then I remembered long ago
How once a tiny child
Whilst playing in a garden
That was overgrown and wild
Had found a tiny flower
Just one, so sweet and bright
And the weeds had been it's cover
From the storm that raged all night
And so I left the path alone
And I let the big weeds grow
For I had been just like that flower
Oh so long ago
And in the garden full of weeds
Alone most everyday
I'd dreamed my dreams and sown my seeds
And watered them with tears
'Til they had grown profuse and sweet
Through those tender years
And in life's garden I grew strong
My counsel kept inside
Now all the weeds well they have gone
But me, I have survived.

CHAINS

It hadn't any walls to keep you in
It hadn't any chains to keep you tied
Yet there wasn't any place for you to go
There wasn't any place for you to hide

The people in your family called it home
They did not share your heart of discontent
For no-one had a dream to match your own
So you remained the only dissident

Now you've found the reason and the rhyme
You get the picture, but it's coloured blue
Now you've found your enemy is time
And missing from that picture, now, it's you.

WAITING.

There's the hat, never worn
Until your hair was gone
There are the walking shoes
That took you nowhere
And there is the coat
Too good to wear
For decades long
You can see
They're well preserved
Look at the price you paid
Yet, there they sit
Although like you and me
They too no longer fit.

NOBODY'S FAULT.

It's nobody's fault
If you don't fit in
If your mammy's too fat
If you daddy's too thin

It's nobody's fault
If the poor boys sin
If the rich man's sons
Seem to always win

It's nobody's fault
If the sun don't shine
If your sibling's still born
If your daddy's done time

It's nobody's fault
The rose dies on the vine
Well that's alright then
I thought it was mine.

NORTHERN LASS

*If I could sleep, I'd dream of a time
Of a kiss and a hug and a sweet nursery rhyme*

*But my home is the street and my bed concrete
As the night vows to be colder
I sit in a huddle close to the wall
Cold in the shroud of a fresh snowfall
The world and a chip here on my shoulder,
Night trains shunting someone grunting
At the child with no childhood
The cardboard box is almost gone
The next one likely made of wood
With handles made of finest brass
To carry this prodigal Northern lass
That would be great, when it's too late,
ME, yes ME, to be carried in state....
...... Shame you have to die,
Before folks can see eye to eye
Oh!...... on that Crematorium wall
I'd love to be a fly
To see them when the curtains fall
How much for me they cry.*

AFTER A LIFETIME

Love promised always, laughter and tears
Marriage and children and how many years?
Everything cosy and now love you find
That after a liftime you're changing your mind

Mem'ries forgotten of babies and toys
The fun we both had with our little boys
Well that's how it goes love it changes us, time
But who could have known you'd be changing your mind

The children are married with kids of their own
It would have been just you and me on our own
I thought we were happy, but I've been so blind
For all of the time you were changing your mind

It's hard to believe that now Autumn is here
You could possibly leave without shedding a tear
Well, go your own way love, if you feel inclined
No use pretending if you've changed your mind

I'll try to be brave and I'll try to be wise
And although it's not easy breaking the ties
That bind us together, I'm hoping you'll find
That one of these days you'll be changing your mind.

I HEARD A VOICE

I heard a voice
A voice from the past
It told me the darkness is coming in fast
The voice of the child said
"Give me your hand
Did you forget me
Do you know who I am?"
And I see her way back
Through so many years
And she's so unlike me
She didn't shed tears
She hated the dark
But she didn't cry
She was an island
She never asked why
She did what she must
And she didn't whine
But she was a stranger
And no friend of mine
I couldn't love her
I didn't know how
I couldn't love her
Not until now
And one night I was sleepless
And I heard her call
I left my bed
And I walked the dark hall
To where she was waiting
That child that was me
I cried as I held her
And we knew we were free.

WHEN YOU'RE OUT OF MY SIGHT

I overheard you say
"I'm leaving, she won't mind
She hasn't cared for me
Not in a long, long time"
But you don't know how I feel
Because you're not around enough to see

Do you know what I'm like
When you're out of my sight?
And I can't give you love
When you're out every night
I feel out of your life
And I'm lost on my own.....

My mother always said
"Don't hold your man too tight"
So I let you be free
And now you're out every night
You're drinking far too much
And I'm angry
That we're losing touch.

I know there's someone else
I'm jealous, so is she
I guess I want to be her
And she wants to be me
Without you she'll survive
But I wonder if you go with her
Will I?

BRIDGE OF TIME.

I lost you in my foolish yesterday
And for the father's sins it seems
The innocent must pay
Those precious days we missed together
And so much we didn't say
Now you've grown and you seem
So far away

I know I played the game of love all wrong
And in another's life
It would have been a different song
Yet blood is stronger than the water
Flows beneath the Bridge of Time
And God knows mine is yours
And yours is mine.

Unspoken are the words I meant for you
Please, won't you listen now
To the wisdom of a fool
Who dreamed a Knight in Shining Armour
Far away and long ago
And still dreams one day
Your eyes will see me so

SKELETONS

When they've been there
All your life
And you thought you knew them
Inside out
The skeletons clink
And your heart sinks
You want the key to let them out
Spring clean your mind
Of times and places
That do not fit
You search the traces of the truth
To no avail
For close to home you find
The more obscure the trail
'Til in the end
You lose your place within the ring
Then stand alone as locked up minds
Frustrate your quest
To let them out
And lay those skeletons to rest

YOUR MIND.

It's a place of your own
Awake or asleep
No one can burgle
It can be your retreat
It's a room, can contain
Whatever you will
Your secrets to keep
Your problems to spill
And when loud is your day
And large it's demands
When you can't get away
And no one understands
The mind is the place
No one can follow
The will may be weak
The heart may feel hollow
But your thoughts are all yours
To share or to keep
It's your independence
No one can defeat
Your mind is a jewel
It's special, unique
Though it can change with pressure
Belie all you speak
When you get to know
And when you are in tune
You'll think of your mind
As that most special room.

THE WRITER.

I know you say you love me love
But I'm hungry for some dialogue
I wish that I could be mistook
For a character inside your book
For everyone that you begin
You fall for your own heroine
You loved the fat, you loved the thin
You loved the catty and the mean
It seems that I can never win
For even at the closing scene
I know as I have known before
Inside your head there's more and more
There is no reason is no rhyme
Why it should wait this love of mine
For you to throw me just one line
Just one for me I can be sure
That you have never used before
Oh once I thought we were a team
When we were young in love and green
But now I wait while you address
While you create and word process
I'll go one of these days or nights
To pastures new and clean
Then you will find I too can write
That famous final scene.

TIME FOR ME TIME FOR YOU

I don't want to talk today
Don't want to talk to anyone
Afraid of things that I may say
Afraid that you may take me wrong
I don't want to speculate
Hurt someone who's been so great
With a careless word or peevish look
So I'll stay home and read a book
I'll buy some chocolate to make me sweet
Have a bath and soak my feet
Do my nails, my hair shampoo
Whilst I dream no chores to do
And when I've spent some time with me
I'll have more time for you

HOME AND FREE

Like a fish out of the water
Never was my mother's daughter
Never ever took a lover
All because of my big brother
And clowning down along the years
Drowning in my silent tears
Watching them as time would pass
Through a one way pane of glass
Seeing all they could not see
Reaching for my family
I found the door, I found the key
Now I am home, I'm home and free
I always cared for them but now
They are no more, I'll care for me

ALL ON AN APRIL EVENING

When love was all on an April evening
When the world had opened up our eyes
We'd welcomed in the bright the new
And kissed goodbye to winter skies
The road was golden with a sign
That said forever, and yet we ran
We were young we'd so much time
Time to learn, to understand
When our dreams were all the same
We were a team no matter what
We were tipsy in the April rain
Now we're the love that time forgot

Well.....here we are on an April evening
And now I know what I must do
I'm going out to find the sun
My April love, my first, so true
There are no rules how it should be
We do not choose how we must part
Just as we can never choose
To whom to lose our hearts
But as I saw last summer end
When the nights grew cold as winter came
I knew that I could not pretend
I knew we did not feel the same
Again it's spring but there are clouds
Up in the clear blue sky
The love birds sing
But soon this caged bird has to fly
And when autumn leaves begin to fall
And these goodbye tears are dry
You and I we will recall
When that love too much
For two, so small
Was all
On an April evening.

PLASTIC FRIENDS

It used to be so easy
When I had one of you
Then when I had two, or three or four
I felt so rich, but now I'm poor
I bought the things I did not need
The price I paid was high
Oh was it weakness, was it greed
I saw I had to buy
With you I bought all that I own
And everything you see
Is had with cash that I have blown
Before it's paid to me
Well, now you are to me bad news
You took my very soul
I'm so cut up but so are you
Now I am in control
You lay before me here at last
Inflexible, in bits
Those credit cards that I amassed
Before I called it quits
Well, as I said, I'm all cut up
And so my friends are you
Oh I can't let this friendship end
Will somebody pass the glue?

THE POOLS WINNER.

He's a lucky bastard
He's won a fortune, just
Now you see the mates that once
You couldn't see for dust
He'll get those begging letters
And calls upon the phone
And women will fall over him
When they find out he's alone
He's a lucky bastard
But he won't give up his job
He wouldn't just be idle
Not for money or for love
Pity that it happened
So late in his life
Never had no family
Shame about his wife
Him and me were always mates
Together we played pool
But he wasn't no great shakes
And he was a dunce at school
But he's a lucky bastard
And he's always been the same
He lost three fingers sawing wood
And they sewed them on again
He's a walking miracle you know
But you never see him drive
Not since his car went off the road
In 1985
He was doing a delivery
Near the highways blackest spot
Well his pick-up was a write-off
And he claimed the flipping lot
He's a lucky bastard
And he is my best friend
And I'll bet his wife comes back now
To help him spend spend spend.........
..........Jesus!.............How unlucky
can you get.

YESTERDAY

Echoes drifting softly on the summer breeze
I see misty shadows through the trees
I hear childrens laughter as they play
I'm standing on the edge of yesterday

Many feet have passed this way before today
Many flowers picked and tossed away
Many sighs have passed the lips of those in love
The grass has grown where lovers used to lay

Many skies haves turned from summer blue to grey
Many lovers came but couldn't stay
Many promised to return some other day
But good intentions sometimes go astray

Many times someone alone will pass this way
Sometimes in September or in May
Like me in a soft and sentimental mood
To live again the dreams of yesterday

THE BRIDGE.

This story's old, how womans' wrath
Did build a bridge
No one could cross
Yet it braved the storms
Throughout the years
And stood erect awash with tears
She was your woman just like me
With all my doubts
And all my fears
Now I'm alone, and so is she
And you are gone so far away
As we walk from the Cemetary
We cross the bridge to yesterday
The air is peaceful, we are too
Because we walk the bridge with you

WHO WAS THE CHILD?

He hurt the child he's not excused
But understand the act
When he was a child he too was abused
He's only fighting back
He didn't know what he was doing
He's so full of remorse
And he's so admired by all who knew him
And he didn't use much force
Lock him away? It would turn his mind
Oh it's such a shame
He's taking the pills it's a difficult time
Society's to blame
It's a wicked world he's done it before
But at least he told the truth
Besides he said he never was caught
Besides he was only a youth
He's turned to God and he's learned to pray
Since people stop and stare
They say "he's an animal. put him away"
It all seems so unfair
He's born to lose, and never to win
Yet he won't bear a grudge
I talked to his family, they stood by him
That did impress the Judge
He's a kindly man so meek and mild
He had the best defender
He never meant to hurt the child
.......Who was the child?.....
.......I don't remember.

A THOUGHT

If there's no shame

And there's no blame

And Jesus did not

Die in vain

There's one question

Must remain

Why has Justice

Such a name?

LAND OF STRANGERS

He was going to change the world
There was nothing in his way
He thought the game of life
Would be an easy game to play
But he was young and blind to all the dangers
And it was lonely in the land of strangers
Until he found a friend
Who took him by the hand
One unafraid of what he did not understand
And he said to that friend
'You see me for what I am
And if I never sing my song
If my story's never told
If I'm not around
To see my peers all growing old
Tell it as it was
The basic honest truth
Don't garnish it with flowers
And mislead some other youth
Who may not find a friend like you
But someone more uncouth
For you told me not to cry
You said'
"But for the Grace of God go I
And in silent understanding
You led me through my darkest night"
But the friend said "No not me"
"I didn't do the leading"
"And what I did you see
It gave my life some meaning
Surely there's more joy
In giving than receiving"
Well your story will be told
Though you never will grow old
Bcause you are a victim of your time
I would like to think
You could have been a friend of mine

HE

He taught me to economise
He said "I've been through the wars,
And I've known just what it's like
To be hungry, cold and poor"
He economised on this
He economised on that
He economised on words
When I longed to have a chat
He said "Do as I do
And I'll show you the way"
And I thought how I would make him
So proud of me some day
He stood so tall, he seemed so strong
So great in my young eyes
I thought "I'll never grow so fine
So clever and so wise"
He didn't spare the rod
He didn't spoil the child
My sometimes distant hero
Always idolized
Yet, even on his love
He economised.

THE ATTIC

*Move the dust and you will find
Mem'ries waking in your mind
Move the dust the feelings strong
Of a generation gone
Smiling husbands with their wives
Pictures of such happy lives
Mothers, fathers, burst with pride
Children standing either side*

*Move the dust and find the lace
The lace of grandmother and Grace
Woven with their nimble fingers
The smell of lavendar still lingers*

*In the dust, the book of prayer
Emmy must have left it there
Full of goodness she was blessed
In the Chapel laid to rest
Move the dust and you will find
The diary she left behind
Times she put her thoughts to pen
Now we can know her once again*

*Every wish, every dream, every prayer
You would write every night through the years
And one by one we all were wed,
And the Chapel organ played
But you remained until the end, a maid
Dear Emmy*

*Move the dust
A thousandfold of dreams delight
Of days of old
All those yesterdays remain
Move the dust
Remember them.*

THE LOST

*She looks into the mirror
Her fingers gently trace
Each line that tells a story
On her tense and tired face
She's looking back a long way
To a naive small town babe
Played a grown up game too soon
With a man near twice her age*

*Oh he was going to save her
He was going to change her life
But she didn't know her lover
Already had a wife
And by the time she found him out
She had mothered him a child
He left her as he found her
On a cold night dark and wild..*

*She left the child behind her
And moved from place to place
Returning to that small town
She'd once left in disgrace
She found a boy from childhood
Who made her soon his wife
Now that seems long ago
Like its in another life.*

*She holds a greetings card
She's feeling sad today
Wondering where the child is
She had to give away
She writes the birthday wish
To loving son, from mother
Then gently lays it in the drawer
To keep with all the others.*

MAGGIE.

A joyride full of thrills and spills
High rides in glider planes
A Sunday down at Hubbards Hills
Where it never rains
That's how Maggie looked at life
And that's why she was more
Because she was the real Mc Coy
No mask she ever wore
She lived her life up to the brim
And never did complain
And still she put so much back in
For such a tiny frame
Came on my scene at sweet sixteen
Seems only yesterday
She hadn't changed no, not one bit
Although it's years away
And through the years gone in between
With someone true to care
She defied, and laughed at life
So she would get her share
She's gone and it's unthinkable
And many tears now cry
For she was not unsinkable
But she will never die.

LILY

I was blind then, now I see
I did her wrong, as she did me
For my man, her son and heir
Was the prize we couldn't share
Almost too late, oh how I learned
But the years had flown
And the pages turned
It was the chapter at the end
I realised she was my friend.

TEARS.

*Supposing we had saved the tears
We have shed along the years
Tears we cried as babes in cribb
Tears for things we never did
Tears from grazes on our knees
Tears from falling out of trees
Tears when we could not be brave
And when we didn't make the grade
Tears of pain from growing up
Heavy dates not showing up
Tears of bad relationships
Tears of sweet nostalgia trips
Grown up tears no one shall see
Tears we shed in privacy
Tears of joy and tears of grief
Tears of anger, or relief
Supposing we had saved those tears
It's just a crazy dream
That the tears of life
Could quench the thirst
Of a world no longer green*

THE BEACH.

I walked alone today
I walked the beach,
And watched the children play
I watched them build their castles high
Listened to their laughter
When their castles fell
What a lesson we could learn from children
The sea was clear
I traced the water's edge
For miles and miles
Tangled seaweed in my toes
Watched the water, the way it flows
Winding, finding it's own way, just like me
I love the sea, I love the beach
Out there imagination grows
Nothing's out of reach
The sand, wet, white, soft, dry
The wind cool, familiar
And flowing in and out, the tide
New and fresh each time
I walked the beach and for a while
This careless world seemed almost fine

SON

I was waiting thinking God
How will he get out
"Oh" they said "If you get a pain
All you have to do is shout"
I shouted, no one came that time
Them understaffed, me overdue
The nurse she said "There's only me
And I've got three as well as you
Find a bed, relax yourself
I'll come in when I'm through"
That first night you gave your warning
Then settled down 'til morning
Took your time, you always do
You'd been with me for all those months
I didn't know you how could I
I thought you were an Alison
Instead you were my Guy
They said "Your babe's alright"
But time moved on and on
It would be three more days and nights
Before we met my son
And when you finally arrived
It wasn't as I thought
I didn't feel this overwelming love
Like we are taught
I couldn't love you
Couldn't hold you instantly, I tried
And when I tried to feed you
Both of us we cried
It wasn't all I'd dreamed at first
For nothing ever is
But I'll never get a better gift
As long as I shall live.

THE PHOTOGRAPH.

What does it matter
If she's getting fatter
Though she drinks her juice in sips
And no sweets have passed her lips
She's increasing in the hips
What does it matter
If she's getting fatter
If her favourite skirt now dips
If it's broken at the zips
If nothing else now fits
What does it matter
I kiss her and pat her
She smiles and my camera clicks
With our unborn child she sits
And me.......well me.....
.....I'm thrilled to bits.

CHILDREN

Oh children of the morning
Dancing through your life
Share your happy mem'ries
With the children of the night.

Some carry a load
As big as a barrow
Live life on a road
Too short and too narrow

Some dance in the sun
Their lives are the morning
Some weather their years
Through the rain ever falling

Yet all wake one day
Grown up without warning.

LETTER FROM A SOLDIER.

You may never know me as I am son
You will only know me
From the stories you are told
I'm not a knight in shining armour
As in days of old
Son, I'll tell you what I am
I'm an ordinary man

I may never see you as a man son
I may never watch you
Play the games that children play
If I don't come back to you
If today is my last day
Always do the best you can
When you grow to be a man

All the words of wisdom ever spoken
Cannot mend a broken heart
But if I can make you understand
One single reason why
Then maybe when you sigh
That I'm not there
It will be with pride
And not despair

You may never know me as I am son
You will only know me from the stories you are told
I'm not a Knight in shining armour
As in days of old
Son, I'll tell you what I am
I'm an ordinary man

I WISH I'D KNOWN THEN

I'm too good to sin
I'm too nice to preach
I'm too old to win
I reach for the bleach
To hide all the signs
Of my mature years
And fill in the lines
As each one appears
My thighs have increased
My hips are more round
My bosoms, not many
You'd get to the pound
But I DO do my best
I try to look good
I've discarded my vest
Like a glamour girl should
I've increased my wardrobe
And I've joined 'The Club'
Eat salads as often
As the cow chews the cud
My number of birthdays
I'm refusing to quote
For who needs reminding
That they've missed the boat?
Yet if somebody asks me
I don't just say nowt
I say young enough to dance
And old enough to vote
I look to my wisdom
And what God did endow
Look back on my youth
My mistakes I allow
If I said no regrets
I'd be lying and how
But I wish I'd known then
What I know now.

SHAG CONNORS

I met him only once
Though I am never sure
He was the kind of guy
You felt you'd known before
As we were introduced
That wall I hide behind
Well it came tumbling down
Like magic for that Clown

And as we said farewell
Could he see in my face
He'd crept into my heart
And found a secret place
I would see him again
There'd be another time
I'd find this soul once more
A little bit like mine

Three months later on
He was dead and gone
I cried the whole day through
For someone I hardly knew
And even now I find
When I am feeling down
He creeps into my mind
That tragic, magic Clown.

BROTHER WONDERFUL

*He fills our lives with pleasure
A priceless treasure
His eyes are gone, no matter
The images are there to scatter
And brighten up the darkest day*

*He's blind
Yet colours beautiful invade his mind
No one with eyes to see
Should speak of beauty hastily*

*His heart
Forever bountiful, forever kind
Is on his sleeve to see
That friends are welcomed readily*

*Himself
My brother wonderful
Who's calm of mind
Who's everything to me
Brings to this life tranquillity*

*Myself,
So full of wonder still
To sometimes find
Those eyes that cannot see
Survey this world so tenderly.*

HEART

How many times have I lost heart

And said I cannot go on

And how many times has a brand new start

Brought me back to where I'd begun

Yet how many times unwittingly,

To someone whose path I've crossed

Someone so much worse off than me

Have I given the heart I'd lost.

BOXES

When we go, to that place higher
Transported as the laws require
Instead of boxes carved and grand
To make an ozone friendly stand
We'd leave in cardboard boxes fine,
They'd all cost fourteen ninety nine
I'm all for keeping this land green
When I'm returned to where I've been
And doing deeds so grave and gruesome
To save the world from bad pollution
But now at breakfast, frail and weak
I pour my tea I cannot speak
I think well it's just up my street
To end up boxed like shredded wheat
And here I am not even dressed
Already feeling so depressed
To think of myself dear, departed
And all my friends so broken hearted
I make my toast and pour my tea
And all I think about is me
Me in one of my posh frocks
Displayed inside a cardboard box
I think of me in my regalia
Apalling bearers,
And their paraphernalia
One each corner praying slow
That the staples will not show
Will it go limp if it should rain
And what of me and my remains
And can the bearers take the strain
Will I be lost - swept down the drain
Or saved by grace of Our Dear Lord
And go back to the drawing board
So I can reach my place of rest
In wooden box of Sunday best
And change before the curtain call
Like Cinders when she left the Ball

*But no, I don't want my Memorium
At the local Crematorium
I won't leave in a cardboard home
Just to create a smokeless Zone
I haven't money for to burn
No, I'll say when it's my turn
To hell with funerals and all that tax
To hell with smokeless chimney stacks
When it's time for making tracks
I reckon I'll just go by Fax.*

WALLS

The Berlin wall came down
We crossed
To find all we had lost
But these were different times
West wasn't best
We'd left the best behind
What came with deprivation
With wealth we couldn't find
Afraid to fail
Another wall to scale
The one between this heart of yours
And mine.

ALL THAT CHRISTMAS MEANS.

Happy families all go home
Dear old people all alone
House with laughter all around
Empty house without a sound

House with colour all aglow
Mother flitting too and fro
Every one in joyful mood
Lots of music, wine and food

Figure in a chair that rocks
Silence pierced by ticking clocks
Flicker of forgotten dreams
Of all that Christmas means

Church doors open, welcome all
Anyone who cares to call
Prayers for Jesus born today
Thoughts of loved ones far away

Everybody takes a seat
Mother starts to carve the meat
Head of table, empty chair
Not as happy as last year

Parties, gifts and mistletoe
Christmas Carols, candleglow
Smiles and tears and hopes and dreams
Of all that Christmas means.

The Visitor.

She hasn't been around this week, bless her
She may not come around again, not ever
But I'm grateful that she came at all
With a memory sweet when we were small
She hadn't changed,
Still as bright, as I recall
She was lovely, dark and slim
I remember everything,
Her smile, her walk, her dark blue socks
(that sometimes went to sleep)
A permanent sore nose
From lots of colds
Bright rosy cheeks

I feel now our affinity
Thwarted by mere chance
I saw in her the other me
Denied by circumstance
I liked her, but at 13 years
She went to sleep forever
Then she returned to me last week
And for days I would endeavour
To seek her in my thoughts
From each dawn until the dusk
Shopping in the Precinct
She'd be with me in the rush
Smiling her sweet teen smile
It was good to go way back
To that place I've been so scared of
For so long and that's a fact

*She had come back all this way
From beyond a star that day
The child I went to school with
But I was not allowed to play
I know she's not around now
But she left something with me
Because I've changed and now
I look at life so differently
And since she left someone has sent
An old school photograph
It was like coming home
To see those faces at long last*

*She isn't on it.............
But she crossed the span of time
To say hello
Now she knows she's not forgotten,
Though she left so long ago.*

QUIET MAN

He's silent he understands
If one's in trouble he lends a hand
He's deep
He sits in his chair apparently asleep
But I suspect he knows
About everyone who comes and goes
He's unromantic
Not the type to cry
Yet if England wins in any feat
I've known him sigh a sigh
He loves....I will never know how deep
For he seldom talks about it
Just loves then goes to sleep
He's strange, he asks for nothing
Except a little of myself
For what it's worth
Yet for me he's the only man on earth
Last night
I saw something in his eyes
Like the flicker of a flame
Just before the fire dies
It really took me by surprise
And should I reach a Century
I doubt that I will fathom
This quiet man who married me

EVERYONE'S A POET

Everyones' a poet
Did you not know
Some may put their life in rhyme
Others need a glass of wine
So eloquent they talk of things
Of strong desires
Of wishes, dreams
Whilst some must speak
By other means
A single rose, without a word
A kiss, a hug, impulsively
What 'eer the message,
You're a poet too my love
As well as me.

EVERY NOW AND THEN

Every now and then
I have to stop
And say to myself
I'm good,
I'm trying to learn
To understand
And be understood
The years have served me well
Though I sometimes feel
I have not moved
Still in the place
Where I began
Still so much
I have yet to prove

This isn't my home, it never was
I never did roam, and I never did fly
Only in my dreams

And every now and then
I have to stop
And say to myself
You're not that good,
You've not seen the world
You see the trees
But can't see the wood
You did not reach the heights
I mean, you had half an education
You do a bit of that,
A bit of this
Your talent
It's a hit and miss

You never reached high, for better things
You never did fly, why didn't you try
Those restless wings..

THE PERFORMER

I've been here before
And I've been here alone
I've had dreams and more
Dreams all my own
I'm standing where the orchestra played
To the good shows and bad shows
Of our yesterdays
But who knows the good shows
And who knows the bad
The critics decide which ones we shall have
Yet true artists abide
Though they're no longer here
In our hearts when they're part of our fine
Yesteryear
Some artists are gifted
From birth that's for sure
It's still not O.K.
They need luck and what's more
If luck that sweet lady keeps out of the way
The fame they are seeking
Comes late in the day
The true artist won't change
He's as hopeful at heart.
When he reaches Autumn,
As he was at the start
If failure's a word that he understands
He still greets the world
With his heart in his hands
Though fear of rejection is with him we know
On every new night
With every new show
He'll reap his reward
When that thunderous applause
Tells him everything's worth it
Because because
We know that performer
Who's staunch strong and true
It's not for himself
Its for me and for you

JUST A PHASE

I am steeped in uncontrol
Splay my feet and bare my soul
Eat all night and sleep all day
Split my zips and cause 'a fray'
Curse too much at others lapses
Take too short walks too many taxis
Indulge myself too much these days
It's no 'sweat' it's just a phase

WAS IT LOVE?

My throat was dry
I couldn't speak
My hands were sweaty
My knees were weak
I gazed at him
Then looked away
I couldn't think
Of what to say
And from his voice
He seemed concerned
I tossed my head
As my cheeks burned
I'd had these symptoms
Once before
Suddenly I felt unsure
Didn't know
Just what to do
Was it love ?
No sad, to say it was the flu'.

THE SEARCH

When there's so much missing
Yet so much there
And you are wishing
That you didn't care
So many words misunderstood
Obscured by shadows
Those parts still good
Easy to see
Other grass greener
The need to be free
No misdemeanour
Save wanting it all
All for yourself
With never a thought
For somebody else

Who would want it all
With no one to share
When so lonely life's journey
On one single fare?

Searching this world
Is some awsome quest
When you are yearning
Your own happiness
You can look to the stars
You can travel the Globe
You can live on your dreams
And watch them erode
Sigh at your imperfections
And gifts that you lack
Like how to be happy
And not lose the knack
Its close I can tell you
So don't turn your back

It's a small light
Just waiting to gleam
It's a small light
I too have seen
It changes your vision
It changes your thought
Split second precision
And all you have sought
Becomes of no value
Now all you impart
Will broaden the landscape
To a fresh start
And the truth you've been seeking
There in your own heart.

THEY SHALL HAVE LOVING

They needed someone today
And Jesus was so far away
They prayed for a hot line to heaven
And somehow somebody heard

Now brighter their colours and whiter their snow
Lighter the hearts that the innocents show
So much to learn, so little they know
They shall have nothing but loving sweet loving
Wherever they go

Leave them their fairytale days
Know them and show them the way
Make their memories so sweet to remember
Sunshine, years from today

Buttercup dreamers never can see
The thorn of the rose
Unlike you and me

So brighter their colours and whiter their snow
Lighter the hearts that the innocents show
So much to learn, so little they know
They shall have nothing but loving sweet loving
Wherever they go.

MIRRORS.

All the mirrors in my room
There to take away the gloom
To reflect the summer skies
Brighten up my morning eyes
There to make my world seem more
Mirrors from the top to floor
I smile in one I smile in all
Morning smiles from wall to wall
But last night I cried and cried
Was like an overflowing tide
Upon reflection I could see
More than I am I wished to be
So with the mirrors top to floor
I fixed another on the door.

HIM AND ME

HIM and me are mates
We've been mates for years
He's always seemed to be there
When I've thought nobody cares
I knew him when I was a kid
Although not very well
But he's the one I would be with
To him my troubles tell
Things I couldn't talk about
He said to me "don't bottle up
Take off the cork and let it out"
I remember meeting him for real
When I thought I was a sinner
Somebody had killed my dog
And I couldn't eat my dinner
I had dark thoughts...... I said "My God"
..... A voice said "did you call?
What can I do for you my dear"
I nearly hit the wall
I told him of my dog
How much he'd meant to me
"I know" he said
That's all he said but oh so tenderly
And I thought "he's not a bad old stick
He's an honest friend for me"
After that I talked to him
When I hurt a bit
When I felt like giving up
And he said to me "don't quit"
I'd smile and I would say "thank God"
And he'd say "it's a pleasure"
I thought I am a lucky bod
I'll keep this friend forever........

*I don't go to his house much
But he visits me
I think he really likes it
He enjoys the privacy
Well his own house is often full
We talk but me and him don't bull
I play his songs and then I sing
Then...... quiet contemplation
With only us just me and him
A sobering occasion*

*Once one of his chosen flock
Approached me in his collar and frock
When I was more than just a kid
He said "Our God will punish you
You know for what you did"
That night I heard God say
"Pray......empty your heart
And we'll blow that pain away"
I told him of the mean words
The man had said that day
Said He "Oh gosh!.. my people
They're losing my street cred"
I saw him clear.. I paled
So surprised at what he said
He said "sometimes we fail
And sometimes we do get weary
And we try to do our best
But sometimes we don't see clearly
Sometimes I long for quiet
While the Universe runs riot
And I know we'll all pay dearly
So I wish someone would hear me"..*

BE YOURSELF

Be yourself, wherever you go
Whatever you see
Be
Yourself

Be cautious, beware
But be fair

Compromise
If you must
But be just

You may falter
You may alter course
But stay true

To all you believe
And when you succeed
Just be you